Waves of Beauty

A series of talks by
Sri Sri Ravi Shankar
on beauty and the Bible

Edited by Judith S. Clark

ISBN: 1-885289-25-1

Quotations are taken from the
Revised Standard Version of the Bible
Editorial review by Joe Puzone and Sherri Silverman
Design by Danny Klein and Judith S. Clark

The Art of Living Foundation
P.O. Box 50003
Santa Barbara, CA 93150

Table of Contents

Introduction   6

Beauty and Love   11

Beauty and Innocence   25

Beauty and Gratitude   35

Beauty and Wakefulness   43

Beauty and Shyness   53

Beauty and Celebration   63

Beauty and the Senses   73

Beauty and Pride   85

Beauty and Luck   93

Introduction

Sri Sri Ravi Shankar is an enlightened master of extraordinary depth and dedication who travels the world sharing his knowledge and wisdom, sometimes in small and informal settings and sometimes in gatherings of thousands of people.

In the summer of 1993, as participants gathered for a course taking place in the Art of Living ashram in St. Matthieu du Parc, north of Montreal, there was lively discussion about the topic for the talks that would be offered each evening. Some wanted to hear about beauty and others wanted to hear about the sayings of Jesus.

The concept of beauty expressed in the Vedic tradition is unfamiliar in the Judeo-Christian tradition, and the two subjects seemed to be poles apart. It was finally decided that the talks would be given on the subject of beauty, but Sri Sri Ravi Shankar always speaks extemporaneously, and as they were given, the sayings of Jesus came into them. A link between beauty and the Bible became apparent. Everyone was satisfied.

$\mathcal{B}$eauty is an inner feeling, an inner awakening. When the negativity and stiffness in you dissolve, then deep inside you recognize the perfection in creation. Waves of beauty, waves of bliss rise through your entire being.

– Sri Sri Ravi Shankar

Beauty and Love

$\mathcal{I}$ have come to set a man against his father, a daughter against her mother, and a daughter-in-law against her mother-in-law; and a man's foes shall be they of his own household.

Matthew 10:35-36

One of the most precious faculties the human body possesses is recognition of beauty. The basis of creation is beauty. In the Vedic tradition, the entire creation is seen as nothing but waves of beauty.

Truth is a quest of the intellect, but beauty is felt by the heart. Intellect analyzes, is curious to know what is inside a flower, how it grows, what season it comes up in. The heart is not bothered with all this detailed knowledge. It simply feels, "Wow! This is so wonderful." Appreciation for beauty wells up in the heart and takes over the whole being.

There is a saying, "Beauty lies in the eyes of the beholder." When you are filled with joy, when you have blossomed in love, only then can you appreciate beauty. A certain level of consciousness is required. When you are stressed and tensed, even the most beautiful thing will appear ugly, or you will try to find some fault in it. When you are hungry or not well, you cannot appreciate beauty. But when you feel wonderful inside, flowers in the grass, even stones and thorns will convey to you the beauty that they are.

Beauty and love go hand in hand. If something is beautiful, you can't but love it. When you love something, you'll find beauty in it. Have you heard the story of Lilah and Majnu? They were lovers like Romeo and Juliet. When Majnu was asked, "If God were to come in front of you now, how would you like God to appear?" he said, "He'd better come to me as Lilah. Only then will I talk to him."

When you love this creation, you see it as beautiful. You become keen—even small details become visible. When you are tired of this creation, you find it ugly. That's why I say that to appreciate beauty, first you must understand love. The understanding I am speaking of is not intellectual, but looking into all the points. See what we usually do: we love something, we find it beautiful, and we want to possess it. When you find something you love, say a painting you appreciate, you want to buy it and keep it in your house. You find a beautiful garment and although you know you will wear it only once or twice, you bring it home and put it in your closet. You have known only one way of loving—love it, possess it, forget it. When you try to possess love, you rob it of its beauty, and then that same love gives you pain. Whomever you love, you try to dictate terms to them. In a very subtle way you try to rule over them. This is a fact! And whatever you try to control turns ugly.

If you don't need a wife, if you don't need a mother, if you don't need friends to talk to, if you don't need a relationship of any kind with anyone, you might consider a Zen method in which only one step is considered essential: the complete subduing of the mind. If you want to walk that path, that is fine. Be alone on a mountain. But then don't long—there can be no longing, no love, no beauty, no relationship, no laughter, no social interaction. If any one of these things is essential for you, then comes the need to understand love.

You have never loved something and not tried to possess it. It begins in childhood. When the second baby comes, the first baby wants all of the mother's attention. "Why did you bring this baby home? Give it away." Many children say that. "You belong to me and me alone." It's a deep *samskara*, a deep impression, this fear of losing our place in the heart of someone we love.

Love which has a fear of loss doesn't blossom. It leads you into other ugly sensations and feelings. Jealousy comes. There is someone you love very much—a friend, a boyfriend, a girlfriend—but his or her attention is on someone else. See what is happening in your stomach—it's churning. You try all sorts of gimmicks to deny what is happening inside you. Much ugliness arises because there is a fear of loss. You never love something that is big, that is enormous, because you have not yet become enormous yourself. And as long as you stay very small, I tell you, there is no joy, there is no happiness, there is no peace. Joy is expansion, becoming big in your heart. This can only happen in a situation where you are very much in love, but you cannot possess what you love.

First comes attraction. When whatever you are attracted to becomes a little difficult to attain, then you start loving it. Have you noticed? If you simply get whatever you are attracted to—just like that, in a second—you don't develop love for it. First a longing must rise—a longing for life, a longing for something more. That leads to love. And when this love matures, it becomes bliss.

In a guru you can't help but see that love, yet you cannot hold on to it. Your mind has an old habit of trying to possess love, so in the process of letting go it may experience a little strain, a little pain, a little frustration. And the concept may come in the mind, "Oh this is not my way. I don't want it." It may be in your makeup to try to withdraw, but that doesn't take you anywhere either. You came to swim, but you only wet your feet and you withdrew. You need to learn a new way to love and still be centered.

The first step is to love God. But because God is so generous, so universal, because God belongs to everybody, the whole creation, all of time, there is no personal connection and love may not happen. Through the guru you see the personal, you find the bridge between the personal and the infinite. Until now your love has known only the personal connection. The guru breaks this pattern. He puts you in such a situation that you are in love and at the same time you cannot possess it. Whenever you seem to be possessive or dictating terms in the relationship, he will turn you in the opposite direction.

The difference in the guru relationship lies in the way the big mind works. It is not sitting with an intention, "OK, let them make a mistake, then I'll tighten the screw." There is no preconceived plan for action. This is very delicate and you have to observe carefully what I am saying. When the small *I* is there, it is sitting and making a big plan—what to do, what to say to whom, and when, and where. All this manipulation happens. But with this big *I*, plans are spontaneous, actions are spontaneous. When the consciousness assumes this dimension, you will see that it will move and *you* are not there at all. There is no *I* there at all. You are just like the ocean, like the sky, like the sun. There is no *I* sitting inside.

Our relationships are very limited and the limitation is always a botheration. So don't expect the guru-disciple relationship to be like other relationships, like mother, father, brother, sister, husband, wife, friends. If you try to make it like your other relationships, you'll get into the same attitude, wanting to possess and dictate. That is why Jesus said, "I'll set father against son, and daughter against mother." He meant he would put fire into people because their relationships had become stagnant and cold. *Fire* means "life." Jesus came to put fire in the world, to put life back in the world.

Some people live as though they were dead, ninety percent dead. They sleep, go to work, eat, gossip, and sleep again. The whole day is spent unconsciously, unmindful of where they are. They are like the frog in the well who thinks the well is the universe, that there is nothing beyond it. This limited awareness is death. It is lack of fire, lack of progress.

The word for "fire" in Sanskrit is *agni*. *Agni* also means "that which moves, which is evolutionary, which carries you further." All the dull, cold relations have to be broken down in order to blossom in beauty. Such waves of beauty then arise in you that life itself becomes a wave of beauty. So Jesus said, "Son and father, mother and daughter, wife and husband—you have formed these relationships, but as time has passed, you have not grown to see divinity in the other person, have not grown to see my Father's divinity, my divinity, the infinite in the other person. You have been dictating. You have been possessive. So it is better that I set you against each other."

This is completely the opposite of other things that Jesus said: "I have come to bring love and peace. I am here as love. Love one another as I have loved you." Amid all his teachings of love, suddenly he said, "I am going to set you against each other." Jesus meant, "If you cannot see the Divine in one another, then I am going to set you against each other. I am going to break all your limited connections. Blossom. Grow out of this limited view. This is not it. You are stuck here." When there is craving and aversion, fighting and possessiveness, there is ugliness. When ugliness comes up, beauty is far away.

Beauty comes in waves. It doesn't remain the same, but comes continuously, as waves do. You cannot practice the appreciation of beauty. There are courses offered in film appreciation. Can anyone teach someone else how to appreciate film—how to appreciate anything? Appreciation doesn't need any training. You need to be relaxed. You need to be peaceful. You need to be free of your feverishness. Then beauty rises in you as waves.

See what makes a child laugh—balloons, bubble gum, cotton candy, jelly beans. Someone brought a packet of jelly beans from America to India and gave it to a small child. When he looked at them, his face lit up and his eyes grew big. What bliss he was in, just looking at those jelly beans! It was as though all the wealth in the world had come in front of him. Even God coming in front of him would not have been more wonderful. Jelly beans...till five, six, seven of them went in his mouth and then he wanted something else, went to a toy. The entire world is nothing but a toy for him.

All your relationships and all this drama are different toys that you're playing with at different times. When you became a teenager, you started searching. "Who was made for me, just for me?" Finally you said to someone, "You are my soul mate. We will be together forever." Now after ten years, it doesn't seem to be right. "We never got along. It was a mistake." Your mind goes that way. And then it asks, "What about the future? What next?" It will be the same story in the future also, because you have not learned to love unconditionally. You have never learned to give space to people. You have never been in love and at the same time been centered. Look into yourself. Then the love in you will blossom, you will become vast and wide.

God loves beauty. God is beauty, and this whole beautiful world is the body of God. Sky is the body of God. Ocean is the body of God. I am the body of God. You are the body of God. You are not just your body; you are the life inside you, your consciousness. You can embrace the sky. You can become the ocean. You are an ocean, so vast is your mind, your consciousness, your being. You're not just this person sitting here thinking, "I'm going to die in only twenty, thirty, forty years—finished." That's not your life. Your life is infinite. You're as old as these mountains and you will remain forever.

If you have studied physics you know that energy cannot be destroyed—the law of conservation of energy. And you are a huge mass of energy. Do you have any idea how much electricity there is in your body? Each one of you could supply electricity to the whole of New York City for a year. Maybe to the whole of New York state! You are a storehouse of so much electricity, so much energy. And you are indestructible, too.

Life cannot be a celebration, cannot be joyful, cannot be fulfilling, if there are no waves of beauty there. At different stages, different things appear to be beautiful, but beauty is not in that object or that thing. It is a sensation, a wave that rises in you which is your very nature. When that starts happening, then you will experience unceasing waves of beauty, continuous waves as in the ocean. The ocean doesn't rest—waves come all the time. And that is enlightenment.

Beauty and Innocence

*J*udge not that you be not judged. For with what judgment you pronounce you will be judged, and the measure you give will be the measure you get.

Matthew 7:1-2

*N*ature has accepted you with all your flaws. Nature never says, "Today you were bad. I'll not give you air to breathe. I'm going to stop pumping your heart." If nature should reject you, you could not be, even for a minute, but nature does not judge you.

This earth does not judge you. You misuse it in all possible manners, but still it doesn't refuse you. Creation does not reject you—not water, nor earth, nor sky, nor this air, nor the sun, the moon, the stars. Breath makes no distinctions; it moves into a saint as well as into a wicked person. Unconditionally creation loves you, supports you and holds you in its arms because it is all Shiva. This entire creation is *shivatattva*, innocence.

Unless you realize this, unless you become innocent, you cannot be one with this kingdom.

Your judgment creates a barrier, separates you, makes you behave peculiarly. When you make a judgment, you are actually judging yourself, but superimposing it on something else. There's a proverb in Sanskrit: *Yatha drishti tatha srishti.* "As is your sight, so is your creation." Your creation will be as you see it. Do not judge.

Your judgment is an impression in your mind. You don't want to be judged, but you judge others. However you judge them, that same judgment reflects back onto yourself, and innocence is lost. This is what Jesus meant when he said, "Judge not that you be not judged." The principle reason why you should not judge is that your innocence will be lost. And when innocence is lost, beauty is lost.

Beauty is not a judgment. It's not like a beauty contest where judges sit and decide who will be Mr. Universe or Miss America. Judging who is beautiful is ugly. Miss America, Mr. Universe—this is degradation. It is like saying love for sale. Beauty cannot be sold. Beauty is not exhibited. Beauty is a phenomenon. Something happens in you—an exclamation, a wave rising in the ocean—that blows the mind away. You're wonderstruck. "Oh, oh!" In that oh-ness, that awe, the mind goes blank. Beauty is an internal phenomenon, a personal phenomenon. If it were not a personal phenomenon, it could not be divine. The Divine is always personal.

If it happens that innocence and pure energy, consciousness, occur in you simultaneously, then that is luck. What is luck? Have you thought about it? When whatever happens around you is pleasing to your eyes, to your ears, to your nose, to your mouth, to your heart, to your mind, to your surroundings, you say, "Oh, I'm lucky!" If anything that happens brings you disturbance, makes you depressed, you say, "It's my bad luck." You can't experience beauty and feel you are unlucky. If you are feeling something is beautiful and you feel you are unlucky, at that moment that wave of beauty has receded.

With the feeling of being unlucky comes jealousy. Somebody else is lucky, but I am unlucky. With the feeling of being unlucky comes greed, anger, hatred—a chain of negativity. I'm not saying that you should never feel jealousy or other negative emotions. No. I am looking into the mechanics of beauty and making you aware of how these feelings are connected to beauty. I'm putting in front of you the phenomenon that is. In beauty there is innocence, in beauty there is total vitality, in beauty there is a sense of good luck.

Question from audience: "How can we be less judgmental?"

First become aware that you are judging and then laugh at yourself for having done it. People who judge do not recognize or accept what they are doing. They see their judgment as fact. "I am not judging. I am just stating the truth. Ask someone else—they will say the same thing."

You are bound to say something about somebody, otherwise life cannot move on. You tend to be goody-goody and talk in sugar-coated capsules. You'll say, "I really like Michele very much. She's my best friend. But..." Why not be straightforward? Why go around it, smearing butter on it, and then saying it? Straightaway say it. Then right in the next moment drop it. Do not keep it in the mind. This could be a step for you toward that point when you don't have anything bad to say about anyone. Without being critical, the intellect cannot progress. But that criticism should not come from the heart; it should come from the throat.

There is a beautiful, legendary story from the *Puranas* about the demons and the *devas*, or angels, churning the ocean of milk. They stirred with a long stick called *meru*. *Meru* means "spine" or "big mountain." They put this stick in the ocean of milk, first tying a big serpent around it. The devas started churning on one side and the demons on the other to get the nectar out. This is a symbolic representation of the negative and positive aspects in the mind being churned by the life force represented by the serpent. When they started churning, the snake spit poison. Even a drop would destroy a person. No one wanted to take this poison. All the devas refused. Finally Shiva came to their rescue. He asked, "What is the trouble? They said, "This poison! What shall we do with this poison?" and Shiva replied, "I will drink it." It is said that when he drank the poison, it stayed in his throat, turning it blue, and he became even more beautiful.

Shiva was the embodiment of innocence. In innocence, when a criticism comes, it comes from the throat. It doesn't come from any deeper place than that. If criticism comes from the heart, mixed with feelings, that makes you bitter and spreads poison around you. I'm not encouraging you to criticize, but if the criticism comes from the throat, not the heart, then it helps you to move ahead and to be constructive. Even gossip, if it is just from the throat, can be constructive. But if it comes from the heart, it is dangerous.

Tomorrow we will look into more of this.

Beauty and Gratitude

For to him who has
will more be given; and from him who has not,
even what he has will be taken away.

Mark 4:24-25

$\mathcal{Y}$ou cannot be grateful and feel lack. The two cannot occur at the same time. When you feel grateful, you feel full, "great-full." When you feel lack, grumbling begins from some corner. If you are grateful, gratitude will increase in you and you will be given more. If you are grumbling, you will see that the grumbling and negativity increase. Jesus said, "For those who have not, what little they have will be taken from them. And to those who have, more will be given. And more. And more." It's a law of nature. For those who do not have this knowledge, there is no way to get out of their grumbling. It becomes a habit. Demand arises and everything is taken away. Even the little joy or peace or love that came into this world with them will be lost. It's very simple.

In India the grandmothers will say, "The sugar jar is full. We will go to the store to buy more sugar." It sounds funny, especially to the children. "If the sugar jar is full, why do you want to buy more sugar?" But the grandmothers never say there is nothing. They never talk about lack. People think they are superstitious. No. In your consciousness feel you have plenty, and plentifulness grows.

This applies to relationships also. If you love someone, know that nothing is lacking. Trust that they also love you very much. If you doubt someone's love, your doubt grows no matter what you receive from them. If you want to be close to someone, first begin to feel that person is already close to you. When you ask people, "Do you trust me?" you are doubting their trust. When you are in doubt about a trust, you grow in doubt, and there is no limit to it.

Whatever is, that grows. If you sow a seed, the seed will grow. If the seed itself is lack, then lack is what grows. Today you feel a lack, and tomorrow you will feel some other lack, and then in a year, even if all these things are provided, still you will feel some lack. Open your eyes and see what you have been given. Then you become grateful. In gratefulness, everything that supports life grows.

When people grumble all through life, their minds don't focus or function properly. Naturally they tend to lose out. That is why it is right to say, "To those who have, more will be given. For those who have not, what little they have will be taken from them." Why is it that Communism failed? This was its great policy: to those who have not, give more and more. And the result was that those to whom so much was given became poorer and poorer. Even on the material plane, when consciousness is flooded with lack, lack grows.

You are fortunate to be given this knowledge, this understanding of consciousness. Consciousness is the power, energy, beauty, and wealth that permeates all of creation. This entire creation is full of life—it abounds in the trees, birds, animals, rivers, and stones. When I say "life," I do not mean biological life only; I mean consciousness. Without it not a blade of grass can move. Without it there can be no progress. Without it there is no beauty.

The Divine is beauty and beauty is divine. In creation there is beauty. Spring has its own beauty. Leaves bud out and everything is renewed. In midsummer everything is green and full. That has its own beauty, doesn't it? And in autumn the color is spectacular as the leaves fall. In the sustaining of creation there is beauty and in its destruction there is beauty.

Playfulness cannot happen if there is no beauty. *Deva*, the word for angel, also means "one who loves to play, one who is effulgent, glorious." Demons fight, men live at peace and gods play. The same force that is beauty creates playfulness also. In professional sports today there is no beauty. The players don't experience beauty, because they are playing out of competition, jealousy, greed—for many reasons, but not just for the sake of the game. "Professional players" they are called. How can play be professional?

The One who creates this universe honors beauty. Look at this flower. No painter could create so perfectly. What color! And see how many different types of flowers there are. If the Creator had no sense of beauty, we wouldn't find so many different varieties and colors in all things.

And see how color and variety are preserved in seed after seed, year after year, age after age. It's not that once it is created, it is gone. This mike, this camera, these lights—what we have created—will not last for thousands of years, but the colors of the flowers here have lasted millions of years and will last for millions of years more.

The very process of maintaining beauty is itself beautiful. Water rises as vapor and forms clouds that rain on the Great Lakes and the Great Lakes flow into Niagara Falls. Without that process, the water would flow down once and then the falls would disappear. It would be like the fireworks on the Fourth of July—they last half an hour and then they are over. But in creation it's not that way. A rainbow comes and then it comes again and again, and again and again. Underneath what has been created with so much beauty, there is a maintenance principal that sustains phenomena through the centuries.

The story of the life of a tree is recorded in a dead log of wood. The beauty of the tree is maintained, even in its transformation. The awards at film festivals go to the actors who show intense emotions like anger and frustration. When children cry, there is some beauty in that, also. It is all-pervasive, this beauty. You only have to wake up and see—this is reality.

Beauty and Wakefulness

And do not seek what you are to eat and what you are to drink, nor be of anxious mind. For all the nations of the world seek these things; and your Father knows that you need them. Instead, seek his kingdom, and these things shall be yours as well. Fear not, little flock, for it is your Father's good pleasure to give you the kingdom.

Luke 12:29-32

*E*very desire arises from the sleeping state. Desire is a product of sleep, yet sleep alone cannot produce desire. Something along with sleep—a spark of beauty in the unconscious—creates desire. Has anyone ever desired anything not beautiful? Has it ever happened anywhere in time, anywhere in this universe, that someone has desired something that is ugly? Impossible. For someone else it may be ugly, but for the one in whom that desire has arisen, it is beautiful.

There are three *gunas* which correspond to three particular states of consciousness. *Tamo guna* brings tiredness, inertia and *rajo guna* brings lack of joy, restlessness. *Sattva* brings light, knowledge, wisdom, joy.

Just a spark of beauty in the sleeping state, in unconsciousness, creates desire. Beauty combined with tamo guna creates desire, and whatever comes out of that desire leads you to inertia. Listen to what I am saying! Every desire, whether fulfilled or unfulfilled, ultimately leads you to a state of inertia. Inertia is a backward journey. You have come out of inertia; you are consciousness. For this reason Buddha declared that desire is the root cause of sorrow. When you have desire for something, you are not aware of your Self, your fullness. Lack of wakefulness is the cause of desire. Desirelessness is not a practice; it is a phenomenon that rises out of wakefulness.

A spark of beauty in rajo guna is the cause of action. The dream state is where you create. One spark of beauty in the semiconscious or dream state is responsible for reproduction in this world. A peacock fans its feathers. A bird sings a melodious song. Flowers blossom and attract bees. The entire realm of reproduction is an action sparked by beauty.

This universe is full of action, yet it is correct to say it is dreamlike because in every moment it is created and then it is not there. In the next moment it is a new creation. You are not here as you were before. The one who was sitting here a week ago is not the same one who is sitting here now.

In the dream state you create. Every dream that you have dreamt, you have created inside this hollow and empty skull. And even as you created the dream, it started dissolving and disappearing. Unless it dissolves, a new creation cannot come.

Creation and destruction are two sides of the same coin. They happen almost simultaneously. The moment you are born you are also dying. You cannot take a breath in and hold it long before you have to breathe out. The in-breath is birth; the out-breath is death. Every time you breathe out you are dying and in every moment that you breathe in, a new person is being born inside you.

Sattva brings knowledge, the spirit of inquiry, awareness. When beauty comes from the angle of desire, it creates feverishness. That feverishness is responsible for action and tiredness, and it destroys beauty completely. In sattva—in awareness and wisdom—beauty elevates. It energizes the spirit of inquiry without bringing feverishness. This is where real joy is found.

Why does one seek knowledge? If knowledge were dry, if there were no beauty in it, do you think anyone would seek it? No, never. If something doesn't amaze, why should one go into it? Why do people work in physics? Because they are dazzled by looking into the atom. "Oh, oh!" they say, "This is fantastic."

A brilliant scientist did well in his career until he reached a point where many people said, "Oh, you must get the Nobel Prize for your work." They pumped him up. One day he came to me and asked, "What has happened to me? I very much want this Nobel Prize, but my work is not going well now. Please do something." I said, "It is this very desire to win the Nobel Prize that is blocking you. You are unable to see things properly because of this feverishness. Your creativity is blocked." And he understood immediately. "Yes, you are right. From the time I started desiring this, I have experienced myself as duller and duller. My work has become very unfulfilling."

Even the desire for spiritual knowledge can be unfulfilling! Out of feverishness you run here and there, learning all sorts of techniques. Some energy, some joy may be built up in you, but then you are pulled by a desire for yet something else and soon you have lost that good state of consciousness. All desire, whatever its nature, is a product of the unconscious mind

When people say to me, "Oh, Sri Sri, you gave a wonderful lecture." I say, "Forget about me. What about you? You also can speak and share this knowledge with others." Or people say, "Oh, the lecture was good, but I can't remember what was said." What makes you weak like this? Your desire, some little desire. The more you are loaded with desires, the more bored you are and the more weak you are. Do you see that?

Strength comes from wakefulness. Remember this! In sattva, the wakeful state, there is curiosity and knowledge, there is something very lively—but there is no desire. Usually we think knowledge or awakening must be dull—if it doesn't have desire, it must be very dull. Buddha must be so dull because nothing interests him; he has no desire for anything. No, no. What makes a person dull is lack of appreciation of beauty.

You are in the dreaming state. If you are sitting here thinking of something, making some plan, you are daydreaming. All your plans are a dream, just as all your memories of the past are a dream, because none of them exist right this moment as reality. You are in a constant dream state—daydreaming and night dreaming—and that is why you are miserable. The awakened one lives in the moment totally—and appreciates the beauty permeating reality in its totality.

I am not deploring any state. I am not saying you should or shouldn't dream. When you listen to me, you have a filter in your ears. In the filter you have put "shouldn't" and "should." Remove this filter. See things as they are. Learn to be with what is now. And what is now? The breath is now. The body is now. It's only the mind that goes to yesterday and tomorrow. So we wed the mind with the breath and the body, with all our sensations and emotions. We observe and watch. This is what we have been doing in our practices today.

In wakefulness beauty manifests in its glory as wisdom, as knowledge. It is knowledge that beautifies an ignorant person. And how does this happen? Through consciousness, through the energy in you. When the energy in you is awakened, when you are able to laugh and let go of the past, you become so light. The practices that we do here kindle that knowledge in you and awaken that beauty in you.

If someone is very dull and has a long face, they are not appreciating beauty. They lack beauty. When you are tired, you cannot experience beauty revitalizing you, that sweet energy bringing new life to your whole system. The power of a wave of beauty is so enormous that it sweeps you away. In front of beauty everything else loses its weight.

For a poor man beauty lies in wealth. For a hungry person, beauty lies in food. For a lonely person, beauty is found in companionship. And for those who are being awakened, beauty lies in the awakening. They say, "Oh! What have I done all my life? Where was I? I was so caught up in small little things, but now my life is beautiful." And the gratefulness that then rises is the most beautiful thing. Have you seen the face of someone who is weeping tears of gratitude? There is no beauty to match that on this planet.

Beauty and Shyness

*I*n my Father's house are many rooms; if it were not so, would I have told you that I go to prepare a place for you? And when I go and prepare a place for you, I will come again and will take you to myself, that where I am you may be also.

John 14:2-3

I am the way, and the truth, and the life; no one comes to the Father, but by me.

John 14:6

$\mathcal{T}$oday one of you said to me, "I am a very shy person. How can I get rid of this shyness?" I said, "Don't get rid of it. Keep it—it is nice. Shyness adds to your beauty. It is your decoration."

Beauty is associated with shyness and shyness enhances beauty. A small child will make a very shy face. When everyone notices, the child may even hide its face. When you feel shy, you become softer and more delicate. But as surely as shyness softens you, shame hardens you, may even make you violent. If you feel shame for something, drop it right away. Shame is part of ugliness, but shyness adds to your beauty.

Beauty, like shyness, is indirect. The way of God and the way of the wise has always been indirect. There is a Sanskrit saying, "*Paroksha priyahi vai deva,*" which translates

"God loves indirect methods." There is fun in that. Poetry is indirect. It is exaggeration. The heart always exaggerates. The mind puts forward fact, but when fact comes from the heart, it is decorated. The heart knows how to put a veil over truth, which then becomes doubly beautiful. The heart may decorate truth to such an extent that the truth is hidden because the decoration has become so big. The intellect tears off all the wrappers and looks into the facts. Intellect has its place and poetry has it place. Fact has it place and decoration has its place. Both aspects enhance life.

Direct expression is necessary if a person is in tamo guna, the sleeping state, but for the awakened, hints and indirect expression are more charming. Partially expressed beauty opens the heart. Love is at its peak when no effort whatsoever is made to express it. Then your whole being speaks that love. I am not saying you should not express your love—at some time you may burst open with it. I am only telling you there is beauty in concealing it. Total exposure is not the language of the heart. Total exposure provokes; concealed beauty invokes.

You love giving what is concealed. When you give a present to someone, you wrap it in many colorful papers and keep it as a surprise until the moment when the present is to be revealed. Many times you hide presents, don't you? You have been giving and receiving presents in this way since you were young. Have you ever thought about what is behind that? Why don't you just give them right away, without wrappings? In the secretiveness and the unveiling, there is knowledge, there is opening, there is joy, there is beauty. These are divine qualities. The Divine functions in that manner in this whole creation, giving you surprises at every step.

Partial exposure is the language of existence. In the night nature takes creation into its womb, and reveals it again in the morning of the next day. As the sun rises you see the greenery, the flowers, all the colors; but in the moonlight, the beauty of creation is just suggested.

See people as more than what they expose or express. What a person says is not what he or she is all about. There is a lot of unexpressed love in each life. In recognizing this, your heart expands. You will never be stuck with what someone says or what someone does. That is just ribbon on the package. If you don't like the ribbon, it doesn't matter. Take the ribbon off. Look inside the package. What is in there? Everyone is a packaged gift.

And there is a place for everyone in the heart of the Divine. That is what Jesus meant when he said, "In the house of my Father, there are many rooms." He was saying, "Don't worry. Don't think, 'There are so many people in this creation, how can I be close to God?' There are many rooms and each one of you will have your own private room."

Something that is concealed, that is out of your sight, that is well wrapped, you may doubt. Then Jesus steps in and says, "I promise you. Trust me. I am right in front of you. You don't know where God is, what God is, but you know me. You know I will not lie to you." As if talking to small children, he says, "I promise you there is a place for you. Otherwise, I wouldn't have told you so. But if you can't believe that, believe I will make a place for you, I will create it for you myself. I am the Son of God. The house of my Father is my house and I will make a room for you. And I will come and take you there."

The mind needs promises. When you love somebody, you want a promise from them. "Do you really love me? Tell me for sure. Promise me." Jesus says, "You know me partially. There is a big part of me that you do not know. You only feel comfortable going to something that you do not know through something that you do know." And that is why he said, "There is no way to my Father, but through me." He meant, "If it were possible for you to reach Him any other way, you would have reached Him by now. If you didn't need me, you would not find me as separate from you. You would live as though 'you' simply didn't exist. But that is not the case. As it stands, you need to go through me.

"If you are inside the house, the door doesn't mean much to you. You don't need to know whether it is closed or open. But when you are not inside, you need the door to be opened for you. And only when you enter the room can you ever sit and relax. You have burned enough in the sun, in the heat. You have wandered all over the place. You are exhausted. You have roamed street after street and never found the water you are looking for. Here, come inside. This room is ready for you. Everything is available here. There is drink to quench your thirst and food to quench your hunger, a bed to sleep on in comfort, and angels waiting to serve you. There are many rooms in the house of my Father. You come. You come."

When one is shy, one needs to be invited.

Let us sit quietly now, take a few deep breaths and meditate.

Beauty and Celebration

*N*ow John's disciples and the Pharisees were fasting; and the people came and said to him, "Why do John's disciples fast, but your disciples do not fast?" And Jesus said to them, "Can the wedding guests mourn as long as the bridegroom is with them? As long as they have the bridegroom with them, they cannot fast."

Mark 2: 18-19

There are two microphones here. One doesn't make noise, one does make noise. In the same way, we have two minds. On one level there is absolute silence and on another level the mind chatters. The more we resist the chatter, the more it increases. Just laugh and let go. If the small mind chatters, let it chatter. How long will it go on chattering before it becomes quiet?

Silence and celebration appear to be completely opposite. Celebration means a lot of noise, a lot of excitement. Silence is the opposite dimension—serene and deep. We'll see how we can experience both these aspects simultaneously and harmoniously— being very silent on one level, like one of these mics, and on another level, celebrating our presence on this planet. Celebration is beauty. Celebration is decoration. The more celebration in a life, the luckier that life is. Eternal life is celebrating every day.

Jesus said, "When the bridegroom is with you, you can celebrate." To be a bridegroom means to be completely decorated. Then celebration wells up from inside. This whole creation is in celebration, relishing and revealing beauty every moment.

All the fine qualities in you that make you beautiful are not in your control. Sometimes you feel rough inside and you ask, "How do I get rid of this roughness?" You may want to do some breathing, some meditation, but also see that this roughness in you will dissolve just in the delicate watching of it. As soon as you observe some roughness, some unpleasantness here and there in the body, it changes and disappears.

There is a story in the *Puranas* of Mother Divine, so delicate, so charming, so beautiful in form, defeating all the horrible, demonic forces. It has a great truth in it. The delicate, gentle observing of what is, of any negativity, makes it disappear. This is beauty.

In another story from the *Puranas*, an *asura*, an evil-minded man, did a lot of meditation and received a boon from Brahma. Whatever he touched would become ashes. His name became Bhasmasura which means "one whose touch turns anything to ashes." He was like King Midas who turned whatever he touched to gold. When

Bhasmasura got this boon, he went around trying to touch everyone he saw. He so frightened people, that they went to Shiva for help. Shiva said, "I only know how to destroy. I do the same job that Bhasmasura does. I don't know how to protect you. Come, let's go to Vishnu." Vishnu, who is very tricky and very shrewd, assumed the form of a charming and beautiful woman called Mohini, which means "one who attracts." When Bhasmasura saw her, he fell in love with her. Then she made an offer to him. "I will marry you, if you will dance with me." He agreed. As she danced, he had to make all the gestures that she made. Mohini danced and danced, making one gesture and then another, until finally she put her hand on her head. Bhasmasura put his hand on his head also, and that very moment he turned to ashes.

On one level this is an entertaining story for children. They like to hear how Mohini danced, going so slowly because Bhasmasura was very cautious and alert, until finally she touched her head and he did the same and burned himself down, but this has a deeper significance. That nature of Bhasmasura represents our tendency to make everything into ashes. Nothing in the world appeals to us. There is no interest in life whatsoever. In such a situation Mohini, divine beauty, wakes us up somewhere deep inside.

Beauty is an inner phenomenon. Beauty is not in objects, not in people, not even in the eyes of the beholder. It lies in the heart of every person. When all the negativity and stiffness in you is burned down, then deep inside you are able to perceive and appreciate the essence of life that is beauty. Once beauty is awakened in one's heart, it spreads throughout the three bodies: the subtle, the causal and the gross. It is the whisper of pure consciousness—pure consciousness tapping the Source, being with the Source. From there waves of beauty, waves of bliss, are created at all levels of existence.

The greater your dispassion, the greater will be your appreciation of beauty. Passion clouds your intellect. In dispassion you are devoid of feverishness. The moment feverishness comes, jealousy comes, anger comes, frustration comes, stress comes, then unnaturalness comes and beauty is overshadowed. It is not lost—it is only overshadowed.

Even in India the usual thinking is that a saint does not care for beauty or bother about nice things. This is a prevalent concept in Christianity also, but with Maharishi that was not the case. [Sri Sri is speaking of Maharishi Mahesh Yogi, who introduced Transcendental Meditation to the western world.] He would attend to every detail—

the choice of a vase for a flower arrangement, the placement of carpets, the selection of wallpapers. In the beginning it was strange and confusing for many of us. "Why does it matter?" we wondered. "Why should we be so particular about how things look?" When he would stay in very nicely decorated hotels, journalists would ask, "Why are you in these nice places? Why do you want all this? You should be in a small hut or hermitage." And Maharishi would simply laugh and say, "Is there any better place? Tell me. I'll go there." He would never explain. If I would wear a plain shawl one day, he would say, "No, no. Wear the gold-bordered one." I'd run back and get it— whatever pleased him. He appreciated beauty, not just things.

The jewel of beauty is surrender. When your mind and your heart are surrendered to beauty, there is nothing to match it anywhere. This blossoming can only happen in the human nervous system. Gratitude, gratefulness, surrender—all these, when they blossom in you, will attract the angels, the devas, the saints. The cosmic beings are charmed by beauty and rejoice in it.

If life seems to be dry because there is no appreciation of beauty there, just wake up and see that you are beautiful. The innocence in you is so beautiful. The dance in you is so beautiful.

Let us have a song now. Let's close our eyes and just swing with the music. Whether we understand or don't understand doesn't matter at all. The music brings us home, unites us. Our minds become totally united in one bliss, one joy, one wave of beauty, one huge wave of beauty.

Beauty and the Senses

*N*ow the serpent was more subtle than any other wild creature that the Lord God had made. He said to the woman, "Did God say, 'You shall not eat of any tree of the garden'?" And the woman said to the serpent, "We may eat of the fruit of the trees of the garden; but God said, 'You shall not eat of the fruit of the tree which is in the midst of the garden, neither shall you touch it, lest you die.'" But the serpent said to the woman, "You will not die. For God knows that when you eat of it, your eyes will be opened, and you will be like God, knowing good and evil." So when the woman saw that the tree was good for food, and that it was a delight to the eyes, and that the tree was to be desired to make one wise, she took of its fruit and ate; and she also gave some to her husband, and he ate. Then the eyes of both were opened, and they knew that they were naked; and they sewed fig leaves together and made themselves aprons.

Genesis 3:1-7

*T*he god of love in Indian mythology is called *Apangat*. The Sanskrit word *angat* means "parts of the body." *Apangat* means "one who has no parts of the body at all." The god of love is called by that name because love itself has no parts, no shape, no form. It is, but it is formless.

Dhanuh pauspam maurvi madhukamayi panca visikhah
Vasantah samanto malayamarudayodhanarathah
Tathapyekah sarvam himagirisute kam api krpam
Apangat te labdhva jagad idam anango vijayate

Note: On this evening Sri Sri's talk sprang from four lines of poetry written by Shankara Acharya, the great 10th century spiritual master who revived the ancient Vedic knowledge that underlies eastern religions.

Apangat is an archer who has a bow and five arrows. Each arrow is made up of five flowers. When Apangat hits you with an arrow of flowers, a wave of beauty is created inside you.

Dhanuh pauspam maurvi madhukamayi panca visikhah
Vasantah samanto malayamarudayodhanarathah

The five flowers represent the five senses. Through the five senses you experience something that is beyond the senses. You experience a wave of beauty rising deep inside you, and your eyes close. You are no longer in form; you have dissolved into the formless. In fact, it is wrong to say you have dissolved into the formless. You *are* formless. You have come back to your nature.

When you look at beautiful scenery, your eyes shut automatically and you sink into that ocean of beauty. When you smell a fragrant flower, the flower remains outside, the fragrance disappears in a void, and you drop into being. That is beauty. It is the same with music. When you hear beautiful flute music, you become fully immersed in it and you no longer know what is being played. You are lost in the formless, limbless divinity within you.

It is the same with the sense of taste and the sense of touch, or sex. Sex, if it takes you beyond form, loses its feverishness. Then *shakti*, the power or energy inside you, starts moving in a new direction. Whatever joy you get in sex, you find one hundred times over in bliss. Bliss has been defined in terms of sex because you can easily relate to that, but there is a difference between the pleasure of sex and the pleasure of bliss. In sex, the other person becomes an object. In love, the other person becomes divine. In sex, your enjoyment lasts for just a few seconds and afterwards you are depleted, tired, even depressed. But in *samadhi*, that very deep state of meditation, you are given energy and long-lasting bliss. It carries you higher and higher until your very presence radiates love. It is good to have this understanding of the beauty of this energy within us.

Dhanuh pauspam maurvi madhukamayi panca visikhah

Every word here is so beautiful—this whole universe is like a bow, and an arrow released from this bow strikes your senses. The objects of the five senses come and hit you like flowers. When a flower hits you, it wakes you up, but you don't feel a pinch. Beauty is such an awakening. Beauty shakes you somewhere so deep inside that you cannot be in sleep.

Listen carefully. I am not negating the world. I am not saying you shouldn't enjoy beautiful things, or that you shouldn't eat wonderful food. Watch a small child going to a toy shop or an ice cream parlor. The eyes light up. There is a sense of wonder. "Oh!" This is a sign of life. If this elevation in life is lacking, nothing really charms you, nothing wakes you up. But overuse of your senses makes you dull. Whichever sense you use a lot, you become duller and duller in that.

If you take a break from this strain on your senses, then you will be able to enjoy the objects of the senses again. If you have been in silence and you hear music, that music elevates you. If you fast for some time, then any bit of food you are given tastes delicious.

Dhanuh pauspam maurvi madhukamayi panca visikhah
Vasantah samanto malayamarudayodhanarathah

When shakti energy is kindled in you, it creates an "Ahh." It's like spring when the entire creation comes up new—the birds sing, trees blossom, leaves come out. And you spring out of dullness, out of inertia, out of your routine.

Dhanuh pauspam maurvi madhukamayi

The wind blows and the touch of the wind brings such a thrill in you.

It's only humans who overdo things. Animals never overeat, never oversleep, never overindulge in sex. They follow their nature. But for human beings everything is an obsession. Your belly says, "No, cnough, I am full," but the tongue says, "Yes, I want it." And so there is no beauty in life.

Creation awakens the senses with an arrow of flowers to create a feeling of beauty deep inside you. If a heart is won, then everything is won in the world. And love wins the heart. What type of love? That which is genuine, that which is true, that which is full of shakti, full of energy. Love can make you feel very weak, but in genuine love you feel energetic and full of strength. That love is total, complete, fulfilling. In the experience of love, all the names and forms dissolve and you are left with one glow.

Apangat te labdhva jagad idam anango vijayate

Because shakti was present, the angel of love spun the whole world. In every love, in every small beauty or joy or pleasure, is the Divine. This is a revolutionary idea. We think that behind temptation there is evil. In the story of the Garden of Eden, the serpent came and tempted Eve to eat the apple which God had forbidden her to eat. The serpent is seen as evil.

You can look at this story from a different angle. A serpent is also considered to be a sign of wakefulness. Maybe God sent the serpent to awaken some energy in Adam and Eve. Perhaps God wanted them to eat the fruit because only then could creation move ahead. When they partook of the fruit of knowledge, God may have pretended to angry because in the face of anger people become more alert. They do their job. Perhaps Adam and Eve would have denied creation for another ten thousand years!

As soon as Adam and Eve ate of the knowledge, it brought shyness in them. Knowledge should bring shyness. If there is no shyness, then we are arrogant and there is no beauty. Beauty wants to be covered, and what is covered is beautiful. Beauty is partial exposure, a partial revealing of the truth.

Your mind, your consciousness, is only partially exposed. It is revealed through your actions, through your expression, through your feelings, but you cannot see your whole mind. To experiment with it—to dissect it and find out what it is—is impossible. You can see just a piece of it, have just a look, and that is sufficient.

Krishna once made a gift of expanded sight to his devotee and friend Arjuna. "You think I am simply your friend, but now I'm going to show you something more. Look at me." In a few seconds Arjuna said, "Oh, you are infinite space." Then he said, "Oh, my God! I thought you were just a friend—a well-wisher and good friend. I have misbehaved with you. Many times I argued with you and scolded you. Now suddenly I see you are much more than that." He said, "This is terrifying, because in this moment I see a thousand things happening at the same time. I see everything dissolving in you, everything being born out of you." And then he said, "Enough, enough. I don't want to see any more of this."

Just look into this moment. There is infinite activity happening throughout the universe. How many people are being born, how many are dying? How many are having their breakfast? How many are going to bed? What is happening within your own body at this very moment? Inside, you are not one person. There is a big township inside you in which many things are happening. In your intestines there are fifty thousand types of bacteria. Many viruses are floating around in your brain. There is a water system, an electrical system and satellite communications. Food is going in and going out. A huge pharmacy is producing chemicals and minerals. All in this one little body!

In that moment when Arjuna saw this huge thing happening, he was shocked. He said, "No, no, no! I don't want to see this. Just let me see your simple, friendly form. Nothing more than that."

Nature is kind to you. From all sides it hits you, but it hits you with a flower and arouses a sense of beauty. Everything appears beautiful. Even thorns. Even a prickly sea urchin. Creation wakes you up and you say "Ahh!"

Malayamarudayodhanarathah

...and with the force of a strong wind, a wave of beauty sweeps through you.

Shankara Acharya's poetry was quoted from a work by V. K. Subramanian titled *Saundaryalahari of Sankaracary* and published by Motilal Banarsidass, Delhi, India, 1977.

Beauty and Pride

"If you are the Christ, tell us." But he said to them, "If I tell you, you will not believe; and if I ask you, you will not answer. But from now on the Son of man shall be seated at the right hand of the power of God." And they all said, "Are you the Son of God, then?" And he said to them, "You say that I am."

Luke 22:67-70

*P*ride is an aspect of beauty. You cannot separate pride from beauty. Have you watched small children when they feel very proud? They lift their chests and hold their heads high. Pride is simply an awareness of power, isn't it? Pride brings strength and steadiness in life. Pride indicates a sense of completion.

All parents are proud of their children because through their children, they feel complete. Every lover is proud of his beloved because he feels complete in that relationship. Every devotee is proud of his master because through his master he feels complete. One who feels incomplete cannot feel proud. For a vine to survive, it needs a pole. For water to fall, it needs a high rock. This completion enlivens the flow of life.

Humility is beautiful, but pride is even more beautiful. Humility is like a vine; pride is like a pine tree, a Christmas tree. They are completely opposite in their nature, but they are complementary and can coexist. It is not contradictory to be both proud and humble.

There is a saying in Sanskrit that too much humility is a sign of cunning. Someone who is plotting ambitiously will show an excess of humility. Yet we trust humility and denounce pride. Why do we do that? Because we know only the type of pride that comes from comparison with someone else. We don't feel proud just for what is, but only when we think, "I am better than so and so," or "I have something that others don't have." This is not really pride.

We think pride is a negative quality because it is often hooked to limited reasoning. We attach our pride to our little talents, our education, our nationality, our religion. "I'm an entertainer, I'm a doctor." "I'm Canadian, I'm Indian." "I'm Muslim, I'm Christian." This pride turns into jealousy and greed and competition.

Pride without any reason, pride which does not require any proof or justification, is beautiful. It is an inner state. It indicates completion, totality, fulfillment of existence.

You *should* feel proud. Pride backs up joy, enthusiasm and creativity in the world. Experience and observe the beauty and power and stability that is pride.

When you are proud, you are confident and you denounce any temptation or desire. Pride does not tolerate desires. Desire indicates a lack of something. Desire is wanting more. Pride is completion, a sense of having everything.

When Buddha was asked, "Are you enlightened?" he would simply smile. Giving proof or reasons is a sign of weakness, a sign of uncertainty. When Jesus was asked, "Are you really the Son of God?" he said only, "You say that I am." How can this be proven? If someone is deaf, you can bring a loudspeaker right to their ear and still they will not hear.

Pride that does not need a proof is real pride. Otherwise pride is just a show. Who makes a show of pride? One who feels inferior. In fact, such a person is not proud. Real pride is found only here and there, not everywhere, and it rises with a huge wave of beauty.

Adi Shankara has described Mother Divine as walking with her breasts high and hav-

ing the pride of an elephant. Fearlessness, a sense of completion, royalty and compassion come together in Her. The feminine quality, especially when personified as Mother, symbolizes humility, compassion, love, caring. When that is combined with pride, it is very beautiful.

Beauty and Luck

*P*raise the Lord!
For it is good to sing praises to our God; for he is gracious, and a song of praise is seemly.

Psalm 147

*Y*esterday we talked about pride. We need to look into it more deeply. Often we mistake pride for arrogance, and those who have arrogance mistake it for pride, but there is a clear distinction.

Arrogance is insensitive. When there is no humility in pride, that pride turns into arrogance. When there is no awareness in pride, that pride turns into arrogance. When there is no love or service along with pride, that pride turns into arrogance. It's the same knife. With just a little twist to it, you can either cut your butter or hurt your finger. Arrogance goes with the small mind. The small mind, being unaware of the magnitude of existence, thinks it's the greatest, the biggest, the highest.

Pride brings joy and in joy there is pride, but if you become insensitive, you get lost in your joy and your pride.

Pride accompanied by humility brings awareness of goodness, of beauty, of one's luck, of one's heart. Luck is a language of the heart. When the heart says "lucky," or "unlucky," it is referring to something that is beyond one's capacity, beyond one's mind, beyond one's abilities. Something that is beyond the smallness of mind, something that is out of reach, something that is enormous, you call luck.

The mind or head knows only facts, while the heart makes everything big. Poetry comes out of the heart. Poetry is exaggeration, and beauty is nothing but exaggeration. There is no fact in beauty. If you try to analyze beauty from your mind, you are gone. And the beauty is gone. Beauty is a language of the heart. The heart decorates, elaborates, exaggerates. When you read a poem, when you sing a song, when you describe something beautiful, it's always from the heart. Analysis and explanation come from the head. Justice comes from the head. A quality comes from the head. From the heart comes only uniqueness, speciality. Everything is made special from the heart, but often we get it backwards. If there is some negativity, we deal with it from our heart and if something is positive, we say it goes to our head.

We exaggerate problems. If a mistake has been made or there is some suffering, some misery, we blow it up beyond its dimensions. If a child has a small scratch, it cries, "Mommy, I cut my finger." It's just a scratch, but it becomes a big problem, a misery. If a few people get sick in a town, we say, "Everyone in town is sick. Everyone is always sick here." We exaggerate and eternalize. All newspapers thrive on this exaggerated negativity, but if something beautiful is happening, they say, "Let's see the facts." They want to look at it from the head rather than through the heart. We do the same thing, don't we? We need to switch it around. When you see a negative quality in someone, analyze it. Why is this person being negative? What is behind it? What does he want? Reason it out. Don't see negativity through your heart because then your heart becomes sore. Analysis of negativity brings compassion in you. An exaggeration of some good that you see brings waves of beauty in you.

You have to take a step to make this shift. If you see one beautiful quality in another person, decorate it, exaggerate it, make it big. Whether that person is beautiful or not is immaterial. Those who exaggerate positive qualities become positive themselves because this body, which is nothing but space, gets filled with praise.

You have been told in the past to praise the name of the Lord. Do this, but not because God is going to be greater because of your praise or that some person will become great because of your praise. No. In the act of praising, *you* become beautiful.

Whenever you have felt a sense of great beauty, that's when you have reached your home, that's when you have been in touch with your Self, because you are so, so beautiful. Whatever beauty you see in the world is only a projection of the being, of the Self—a glimpse of Self.

When you rejoice in beauty, the entire creation rejoices with you. The very purpose of such variety in this creation is to bring you back to your Self, to come to know that you are beautiful—that you are beauty. And in that bliss, all that you need, all that you would want will simply keep happening. It's beautifully described in a verse by Adi Shankara:

> *Sudhasindhor madhye suravitapivati parivrte*
> *Manidvipe madhye...*

On a small island in an ocean of milk is a wish-giving tree

Sudhasindhor madhye suravitapivati parivrte
Manidvipe nipopa ... cinta manigrhe
Sivakare mance paramasiva paryankanilayam...

Beside the wish giving tree is a beautiful house called *chintamani*. *Chintamani* means "awareness, wisdom." In the house is a couch. "On the couch of Shiva, O Mother, you are sitting and smiling. Who can worship you? Someone who is not lucky cannot worship you. Who can adore you? Only those who are lucky."

To experience beauty you need to be lucky. Again, never think of luck in terms of justice or in terms of your analytical mind. It is just an expression of the heart. When one realizes, "I could not do it by my mind, by intellect, my abilities, my capabilities. What has come to me is beyond my comprehension, my wildest imagination," then one says, "I am lucky."

The ocean of milk signifies plenitude. When you feel lack, you experience the desert, but the ocean is a sign of abundance. Consciousness is often referred to as an ocean of milk. When there is a sense of abundance in our own consciousness, amidst that abundance is the wish-giving tree. The wish-giving tree represents what is called *siddhis*—a state in which whatever you need comes to you. And in the midst of that, you find *chintamani*—discrimination, knowledge, wisdom. In chintamani, the house of discrimination, there is total alertness, sharpness of intellect, awareness, wisdom. Inside that house is *Shiva-karamancha*, the couch or bed, that is innocence and inner wisdom. On that bed of innocence, of purity, of transcendental bliss, lies the power of creation. *Shakti*, the life force, resides in that innermost core. The secret and spiritual glory resides there. This could have been said analytically, but instead the poet has given us such a beautiful image.

All right, now we will look at some of the questions in the basket.

The Art of Living Foundation in the United States and similar organizations around the world offer programs, workshops and educational materials as an introduction to the teachings and techniques of Sri Sri Ravi Shankar.

For information on Art of Living courses or to locate an Art of Living Center in your area, contact:

Art of Living Foundation
Post Office Box 50003
Montecito, CA 93150
805-563-6396

Or visit the Web site at:
http://www.artofliving.org

To purchase books and recordings or obtain a catalog, contact:
Art of Living Books and Tapes
800-574-3001